Enjoy the Book!

Steve

# Just Sayin 2021:
# A Perspective in Rhyme

by Steve Rosen

PITTSBURGH, PENNSYLVANIA 15238

The contents of this work including, but not limited to, the accuracy of events, people, and places depicted; opinions expressed; permission to use previously published materials included; and any advice given or actions advocated are solely the responsibility of the author, who assumes all liability for said work and indemnifies the publisher against any claims stemming from publication of the work.

All Rights Reserved
Copyright © 2022 by Steve Rosen

No part of this book may be reproduced or transmitted, downloaded, distributed, reverse engineered, or stored in or introduced into any information storage and retrieval system, in any form or by any means, including photocopying and recording, whether electronic or mechanical, now known or hereinafter invented without permission in writing from the publisher.

RoseDog Books
585 Alpha Drive
Suite 103
Pittsburgh, PA 15238
Visit our website at *www.rosedogbookstore.com*

ISBN: 979-8-88527-907-9
eISBN: 979-8-88527-955-0

# Just Sayin
# 2021:
# A Perspective in Rhyme

# Table of Contents

I'm Not Ready to Write Our Obituary . . . . . . . . . . . . . . . 3

Get Real; Republicans Aren't Changing . . . . . . . . . . . . 6

No Surprise; He Walked. . . . . . . . . . . . . . . . . . . . . . . . . 8

Do You Need to Be Connected to Get Injected? . . . . . 13

Ted, Really? . . . . . . . . . . . . . . . . . . . . . . . . . . . . . . . . . 17

Senators Three . . . . . . . . . . . . . . . . . . . . . . . . . . . . . . . 19
(To the children's poem "Three Blind Mice")

A Biden Campaign Promise . . . . . . . . . . . . . . . . . . . . . 23
(To the tune "Old McDonald Had a Farm")

Say It Ain't So, Andrew . . . . . . . . . . . . . . . . . . . . . . . . 25
(To the tune "Where Have All the Flowers Gone?")

COVID, Please Just Go. . . . . . . . . . . . . . . . . . . . . . . . . 28

Vaccination Passport Blues . . . . . . . . . . . . . . . . . . . . . 30

The Liz Cheney Question . . . . . . . . . . . . . . . . . . . . . . . 33

Israeli-Palestinian Conflict Explodes Again . . . . . . . . . 35

Fauci – The Real Villain?. . . . . . . . . . . . . . . . . . . . . . . 39

Is the Filibuster Rule Just an Evil Tool? . . . . . . . . . . . . 41

Infrastructure Bill, Any Chance? . . . . . . . . . . . . . . . . . 45

Anti-Vaxxers, Not Helping . . . . . . . . . . . . . . . . . . . . . 49

Apartheid, U.S. Style . . . . . . . . . . . . . . . . . . . . . . . . . . 52

"Andrew Two" – So Sad; You're Through . . . . . . . . . . . 54

Will Delta Be The Worst?/Will Boosters Save The Day? . 56

Afghanistan – The U.S. Is on the Run . . . . . . . . . . . . . . . 59

Texas – You've Misread America's Pulse . . . . . . . . . . . . 62

Infrastructure/Debt Ceiling – My Patience Tried . . . . . . . . 65

An Early Test of the 2022 Elections . . . . . . . . . . . . . . . . 67

Post-Election and Looking Ahead . . . . . . . . . . . . . . . . . . 70

One Final Note . . . . . . . . . . . . . . . . . . . . . . . . . . . . . . . 76

# I'm Not Ready to Write Our Obituary

So, it's just the beginning of January,
And many pundits are writing our obituary.
Sure, there is plenty of cause for concern;
Have we reached a point of no return?

The Georgia Senate elections were a moment of hope,
Perhaps signaling Trump's reign at the end of its rope.
The electoral vote count required Congress to act
And certify Biden's election as a matter of fact.

But history will show that Trump was not done,
And shamefully, he was not the only one.
Republican lawmakers continued to spread his lies;
Their re-election hopes, to his coattails, were tied.

Trump pressured Pence to unilaterally change the votes;
He refused and was labeled TRAITOR and turncoat.
Several Republican Congressmen stepped up to the plate
And challenged the results and demanded a debate.

Meanwhile, Trump loyalists promised to create a storm.
To Washington en masse, they promised to swarm.
A rally of thousands was organized on the Mall,
And a march to the Capital ended in a free-for-all.

Trump, his kids, Rudy—all spoke, inciting the crowd:
"Be strong, not weak"; "fight"; and be "Boys Proud."
The horror of that day unfolded for the world on TV:
Capital breached, police maimed, killed—a terrorist spree.

But Congress was determined to fulfill its obligation,
Reconvened that night holding the world's attention,
And despite the horrific events earlier that very day,
Republican members tried to halt the vote anyway,

Telling lies that underpinned the frustration of the mob,
The lies Trump told over again—that he was robbed;
The very lies that were debunked again and again
By the states, the courts…Trump soundly didn't win.

Biden's win that night, Congress eventually certified,
But the events that day left most Americans horrified
With many questions that should be reasoned through
And so very much healing, Biden's team must do.

Questions like, why were the authorities so unprepared?
Should Trump be punished? Or, as some suggest, spared?
Would impeachment make sense with just 10 days to go?
Or would it only serve to further divide…? I just don't know.

Alt-right militia groups have cast the country in a pall.
Pelosi is committed to impeach; is that really a good call?
There is chatter of further disruption on Inauguration Day,
More evidence this divided country may have lost its way.

But through it all, this is why I still have hope
That our democracy is not headed down a negative slope.
We've shown that the power of the vote is stronger than ever,
And the country is embarking on a peaceful transfer of power.

Who knows what good Biden's administration will bring?
But the very fact of its existence is an important thing.
That Americans can vote and the majority has its way
Is proof America's obituary should be a long way away.

# Get Real; Republicans Aren't Changing

So, today is just January twenty-fifth;
This story I'm telling you won't give you a lift.
Just days since rioters stormed those hallowed halls,
Should have ushered in Trump's end once and for all.

That stormy day, Congress certified the Biden/Harris win,
A new admin most Americans were happy to see begin.
When the alt-right threatened further violent acts,
Twenty-five thousand troops guarded D.C. to chill any attack.

A second Trump impeachment was quickly in hand;
Republican House members made a symbolic stand.
Only a very few, just a hand full, voted yes;
All the others voted no—a result not surprising to guess.

Would 17 Republican Senators vote to convict?
Democrats were hopeful that number would do the trick.
But as the days since impeachment continued to pass,
The number of possible yes votes have decreased, alas.

It now appears unlikely there will be a conviction,
And as of this writing, sadly, that is my prediction.
The burning question to be asked and answered is this:
How could what should have been a certainty go amiss?

All members of Congress were victims and terrified on 1/6;
They all blamed Trump for putting them in that terrible fix.
But Trump nonetheless still holds a tight grip on his base,
That is the reality every Senator voting had to face.

It seems political survival outweighed the oath they took:
A yes vote would be devastating to their re-election outlook.
Dems in the Senate will still hold the trial and record the vote,
So that of each Republican vote, history will take note.

As we wait for Trump's impeachment trial to commence,
The sides are drawn; the outcome holds little suspense,
Notwithstanding that each day uncovers more evidence
That, for Trump's election lies and actions, there's no defense.

Brought to light were his efforts to have his DOJ intervene,
To threaten Georgia to assist in his election fraud scheme;
His supporters both in the House and on the Senate side
Worked to rewrite history and justify his and their lies.

When Senate election campaigns start in earnest next year,
Remind voters their Senator's devotion to Trump—not them—is clear.
Will that be a strong enough reason to change voters' minds?
Sadly, there won't even be a handful of switchover votes one finds.

# No Surprise; He Walked

Trump's second impeachment trial has ended;
His behavior was shockingly badly defended.
In the end, it seemed no real defense was necessary;
To Republican Senators, his guilt was only secondary.

The House trial managers presented an amazing case—
Tweets, speeches, and videos proved Trump a disgrace.
Nonetheless, most Republican Senators voted to acquit,
Fabricating a technicality, his guilt they refused to admit.

Trump's base steadfastly continues to believe his "big lie."
Biden stole the election; Trump's "win" they must rectify.
And Republican leaders choose to stand with Trump
To avoid, in the next round of elections, being dumped.

It's possible the courts may be next to pick up the fight.
Facts of Trump's bad behavior daily are coming to light.
Impending are federal and state election tampering cases
As well as civil and criminal cases in a number of places.

Nancy Pelosi has called for a 9/11 style commission
In part to unearth the alt-right's ties to this politician,
To identify why on 1/6 so many things went wrong
And why the Capital was so vulnerable to that throng.

Many feared an acquittal would just embolden Trump;
During the trial, it appeared he quietly sat on his rump.
But seeing Republicans and his base come to his defense
Has emboldened Trump to again go on the offense.

McConnell's post impeachment trial speech added fuel,
Calling Trump's behavior criminal and an alt-right tool.
Trump minced no words at all in quickly lashing back,
Calling McDonnell dower, weak, and a political hack.

State Republican parties have behaved with no shame,
Censuring their "traitor" Senators, finding them to blame.
Burr, Cassidy, and Toomey have all been called out;
Voting "truth" it seems was not what their job was about.

Biden is determined to focus on his administration's plans
And not have his goals derailed by Trump's shenanigans.
The "Trump Party" is positioned to remain a formidable foe.
Should Biden ignore Trump or fight him toe to toe?

While pondering that question, consider these scary facts:
Republicans have stepped up their voter suppression attacks;
Using the big lie, a stolen election, as their suppression excuse,
States have turned their state legislators alarmingly loose.

Since January first, 33 states have proposed 150-plus suppression bills,
Citing voter fraud as the villain and cause of all their supporters' ills.
Rather than trying to sway voters to their causes with facts,
They aim to suppress the right to vote with baseless attacks.

I know Biden's focused on his agenda, the first hundred days,
But the House and one-third Senate elections are two years away.
If he wants lasting success, he must also focus serious attention
To safeguarding voter enrollment, retention, and fair elections.

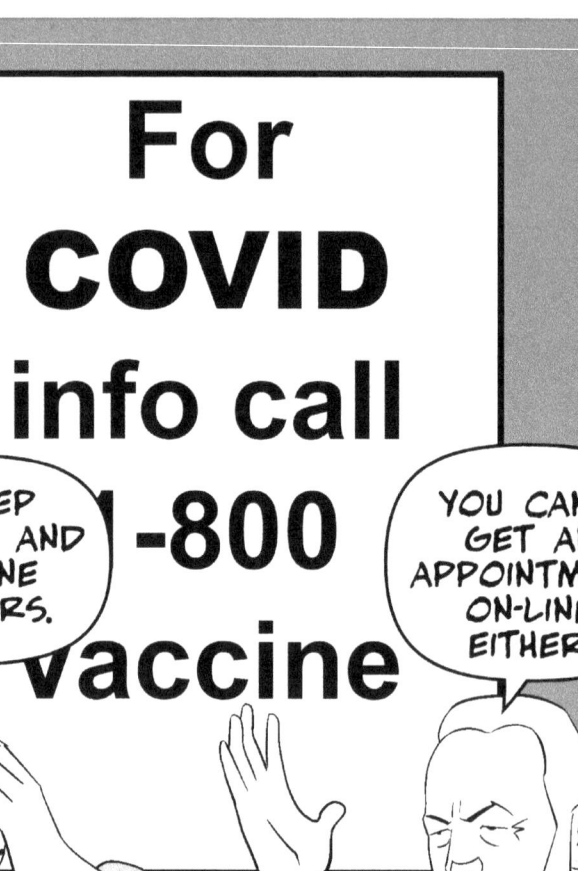

## Do You Need to Be Connected to Get Injected?

It seems you need to be connected to get injected,
Or put another way, favored to be inoculated.
The Coronavirus vaccines are real and here,
But not available to everyone equitably, I fear.

I have no problem with establishing a priority list.
In fact, on such a list, the government should insist.
But it seems from the rollout's very beginning,
The facts and the goals were quickly separating.

Pent up demand for a vaccine was immense;
Expectations were sky-high for their rapid dispense.
The federal government added fuel to the fire
By releasing numbers that proved them to be liars.

States were expected to establish individual plans;
Get those done just as soon as they possibly can.
No state wanted to miss out on its vaccine allocation
And be left to deal with its citizens' frustrations.

A complication was the Pfizer vaccine's limitations,
Requiring sub-zero temperature for its storage duration.
That meant only a very limited number of storage sites
In each state were equipped to do the storage job right.

Twenty million shots were promised by the end of December;
Less than 3 million given by the end of 2020, if you remember.
In addition to the pent up demand caused by that
Were reports of jumping lines, lying, using any clout.

Some vaccines went bad due to lax storage procedures.
Why so hard to maintain a temperature in a freezer?
The elderly waiting in long lines for hours for their shot
Finally told, "Sorry, unfortunately we've run out of that lot."

To counter mistrust among some in the population,
Known celebrities were dosed early in TV presentations
But why was Congress among the first in line
When many of them are young, healthy, and doing fine?

Doctors' offices have no information when you call;
It's like they never knew a vaccine was coming at all.
Phone numbers posted by the state to call for a date
Go unanswered or tell you be patient and wait.

Maybe the new administration will right the ship;
We need to give the current crew a rejection slip.
Meanwhile, my wife is constantly driving me crazy—
If I can't get us a vaccination date, it's proof I'm just lazy!

# Ted, Really?

There once was a Senator from Texas
Who by all accounts was quite senseless.
He slinked out of town,
Left Snowflake alone, lying around,
No punishment too harsh was the consensus.

You see, a winter storm had hit his state;
He blamed his escape partly on his mate.
So to Cancun, he ran,
Leaving Texas with no plan.
Such a cowardly reprobate.

Ted also blamed it on his daughters,
Claiming they begged for sun and warm waters.
So to Cancun he fled,
Leaving Texas in dread,
Half the state with no heat and no water.

Police escorted his family to the plane;
They must have thought the request was insane.
A weekend at the Ritz Carlton
Of all the glitzy places to run,
On a Senator's salary, he's got a lot to explain.

Once there, he realized his mistake
Only because the media made it a news break.
He booked the next flight,
Hope he didn't sleep well that night.
Ted, there are some things you just can't remake.

The guy most affected by Ted's blunder
Was New Jersey's ex-governor; no wonder—
Ted's escapades brought to light
What Christy did was also not right.
He too abandoned his state during a disaster.

Ted and Chris both have ambitions;
Presidential bids are their future missions.
Let me say, I for one
Hope they're both finally done.
Neither has the right qualities for the position.

# Senators Three

*To the children's poem "Three Blind Mice"*

Senators. Senators.
Three Senators. Three Senators.
Hawley, Cruz, and Graham by name,
Building their legacy of lasting shame.
How very despicable they became,
Those three Senators.

Lindsay Graham. Lindsay Graham.
Trump's Senate man. Trump's Senate man.
He pressured Georgia to change their choice,
There to lend Trump a supportive voice.
If Trump had won, he would have surely rejoiced,
Trump's Senate man.

Josh Hawley. Josh Hawley.
Claimed election fraud. Claimed election fraud.
He voted to not certify Biden's win,
Just one of his many obstructionist sins.
In Senate riot hearings, he was at it again.
Why? Josh Hawley.

Lying Ted Cruz. Lying Ted Cruz
See how he runs. See how he runs.
He fled Texas to avoid the storm;
Embarrassing behavior is just his norm.
Is that the way for a Senator to perform?
You're caught, Ted Cruz.

They're not alone. They're not alone.
Two best for last. Two best for last.
McCarthy lives to kiss Trump's ass.
Every Trump sin, McCarthy gives a pass.
Does he really expect this love fest to last?
Just no backbone.

Ron Johnson. Ron Johnson
Must watch Fox News. Must watch Fox News.
Could one man really have so much hate?
His stupidity is beyond any debate.
The man is an unforgivable reprobate;
Just nuts, Ron Johnson.

Now I'm done. Now I'm done.
I've had some fun. I've had some fun.
But isn't their behavior really so sad?
How could five Congressman be so bad?
I'll tell you the truth; they make me so mad.
Vote them out, each and every one!

# A Biden Campaign Promise

*To the tune "Old McDonald Had a Farm"*

The Dems passed the Biden Bill;
A huge win it was.
The opposition tried to stand its ground,
Causing quite a fuss.
McConnell called his troops to arms.
This bill will cause great harms,
So he quack-quacked here
And he quack-quacked there,
But the Dems passed the Biden bill
For the country, quite a plus.

Quite a lesson for the Dems,
Despite the win it was.
Republicans would go to great lengths
Any time to make a fuss.
Johnson insisted the bill be read,
A lame attempt to see it dead,
So the staff quack-quacked here,
And they had to quack-quack there,
In his lame attempt to thwart the Dems.
So sad a thing it was.

No Republican voted, "Yea,"
Despite the popular appeal,
Claiming if passed the deficit would rise
And it was a harmful deal.
So they lied so here,
And they lied so there.
Here a lie; there a lie—
Everywhere a lie lie.
No Republicans voted, "Yea";
Maybe their fate is sealed.

The filibuster must surely go;
It's time it goes away.
Still so much work for the Biden team,
Can't delay another day.
Infrastructure here,
And the green agenda there,
With House obstruction here,
And Senate obstruction there,
The filibuster stands in the way;
Change that rule today.

# Say It Ain't So, Andrew

*To the tune "Where Have All the Flowers Gone?"*

Where have all your supporters gone?
Your time is passing.
Where have all your supporters gone?
Yours, not so long ago.
Where have all your supporters gone?
Gone to safer bets, each and every one.
Seems you have few or none;
Seems you have few or none.

Why have all your supporters gone?
Deserted you so quickly.
Why have all your supporters gone?
The feeling is, you're icky.
Why have all your supporters gone?
Five accusers have spoke up.
They have you on the run;
They have you on the run.

Lindsey Boylan was the first,
Quite the landmine.
Lindsey Boylan was the first,
Said you crossed the line.
Lindsey Boylan was the first,
How quickly she—not you—was believed.
Still a few said, "Let's wait and see."
A few said, "Let's wait and see."

Charlotte Bennett outed next,
Meat now on the bone.
Charlotte Bennett outed next,
More and more you're alone.
Charlotte Bennett outed next,
Denials won't make it go away.
Calls demanding that you go;
Most folks want you to go.

Anna Ruch was next up to bat;
Three strikes means you're out.
Anna Ruch was next up to bat,
Calling you a lout.
Anna Ruch was next up to bat,
Lititia James now in the act.
Investigation on,
Investigation on.

Karen Hinton, Ana Liss…
It's becoming the norm.
Karen Hinton, Ana Liss…
It's now quite the storm.
Karen Hinton, Ana Liss…
Impeach him now is the call.
Andrew, maybe give it up;
Andrew, just give it up.

For me, the jury is still out;
Let's air all the facts.
For me, the jury is still out;
Investigate, not attack.
For me, the jury is still out;
Consider all the good he's done.
Is that not the prudent tact?
Is that not the prudent tact?

# COVID, Please Just Go

Here we are, nearing the middle of 2021.
The Coronavirus still has us on the run;
The J and J vaccine was just put on pause.
Let's hope it's not just another lost cause!

Europe is still struggling in the virus's grip;
Few in the U.S. are planning a foreign trip.
And below the equator it's well into fall,
Their winter is likely to be the worst one of all.

At home, the UK strain has become dominant,
And the Indian strain may prove more resilient.
It's looking more like we'll need booster shots;
An annual one, same as the flu, like it or not.

Several U.S. states have cases on the rise;
To no one should that really be a surprise.
We're in a race—vaccinations vs. mutations.
Herd immunity requires dosing 70 percent of the nation.

As of today, we're a long way from that goal;
Less than 50 percent of the nation as a whole.
Vaccine deniers make that goal difficult to achieve;
Excuses aside, their reluctance is hard to believe.

A year in, and there is still so much we don't know.
Will vaccines remain effective, cause mutations to slow?
Can children safely be given any of the vaccines?
Is it important to regularly have children screened?

More and more activities are opening this spring;
Attendance at sporting events now a common thing,
And though sports teams adopted strict protocols,
Many schools and leagues have had games called.

It's the same tug of war debated for a year or so:
To open things up or apply breaks and go slow?
States flip flopping between open and closed;
The more things open, the more chance we're exposed.

Folks are weary of cautions like wearing masks;
Social distancing has become a tiresome task.
The tug between economic and social forces
Aids the virus more than we benefit from choices

It appears the new normal the virus may bring
Looks more like it could be a permanent thing.
I just hate to think that it could be here to stay;
We should all do what it takes to make it go away.

# Vaccine Passport Blues

A vaccine passport, what a useful tool!
Preventing its use would be a reckless rule;
To require one has become a raging storm,
Again, that has Reds and Blues quite torn.

When you're vaccinated, you get a card;
A document to be saved—don't discard!
Take a snapshot of it on your phone,
Make copies, and laminate one you own.

For folks who have received the shot,
They're proud, relieved, boast about it a lot.
But for those still refusing to get onboard,
This requirement really strikes a bad chord.

The same folks who resist wearing a mask,
A requirement seemingly too much to ask,
But they buckle up when they get in their car,
Headed around the block or someplace far.

The findings of experts strongly suggest
Vaccinated folks know a passport is best.
There is comfort knowing others in their space
Have proof of the shot and mask their face.

Many schools and offices require documentation,
Barring admission without proof of vaccination.
Some develop their own form of a passport,
Ensuring a mechanism for folks to report.

A number of apps are being developed;
Vaccination certificates on them to be uploaded,
Digitized into a standard data format saver,
Recording vaccination proofs, testing, and waivers.

Other countries have established strict rules
And utilize vaccination and testing tools.
To guard U.S. entry, we have so far fallen short,
Requiring only a negative current test report

The Administration is frustrated by the doubters' stance;
The doubters want the economy to advance
But refuse to take steps to safely allow reopening—
Vaccinations, masking, and safe distancing.

Republican obstruction has not reached its limits;
Bills that would mandate passports, they prohibit.
In some states, they have moved to strike first,
Banning all mandates and making things worse.

From the very beginning of this COVID pandemic,
Our cultural divide has prolonged this epidemic.
Obstruction is harmful, senseless, and sad.
Writing this doesn't help; it makes me so mad!

# The Liz Cheney Question

So this seems to be the question of the day:
Can Republicans make Liz Cheney go away?
She's the sole Wyoming Congressional Rep,
But to her leadership, she's moved out of step.

Maybe the real question is, should they dare
To remove her from her leadership chair?
McCarthy is trying to sell, "No one will care,"
But others, like Romney, warn them to beware.

So what exactly is all the Cheney fuss about?
It's about the "Big Lie," there is no doubt.
She has been outspoken, refusing to go along,
Forcefully stating the Big Lie myth is all wrong.

And what, you ask, exactly is the Big Lie?
Biden stole the election, and it must be rectified.
At all cost, restore Trump to his rightful assent
As the legitimate and rightful U.S. President

So why am I writing about this today?
Well, today is Tuesday, the eleventh day of May.
Tomorrow, the Republicans in the House will vote;
Liz keeping her leadership chair seems remote.

Think about where we are; the middle of May
And still the Big Lie myth won't go away.
Voter fraud was debunked, leaving little debate,
Yet recounts are underway in a number of states.

The Republican agenda seems to boil down to two:
Thwart the Democrats' agenda with whatever they can do;
Use the Big Lie to agitate and motivate the base
To win every 2022 House and Senate race.

Will the Cheney vote be a McCarthy/Trump win?
Either a win or a loss may see their downfall begin.
A win will turn moderate Republicans further away;
A loss will signal hope for a brighter day.

# Israeli-Palestinian Conflict Explodes Again

I realize that reporting on this conflict is big news;
Between facts and opinions, it's facts you must choose.
Soundbites from politicians on one side or the other
Mostly has me sighing and/or shouting, "Oh brother!"

Israel has been fighting for its survival for 75 years,
Conflicts and wars and shedding so many tears,
From humble beginnings with enemies on all sides
To a modern democracy with well-earned national pride.

And peace has been reached with a number of foes;
Maybe a fragile peace at best, as those things go,
But you take progress wherever you can
And work toward a lasting regional peace plan.

But peace with all groups has not been a success.
Relations with the Palestinians are still a mess
Complicated by population, geography, and religion;
It's been built up over years of mutual hatred and division.

Politics is a huge factor in fueling the current conflict:
Netanyahu appeasing the far-right religious sect;
Hamas seeing weakness in the Palestinian Authority;
All factors in producing the current catastrophe.

Netanyahu wants to eliminate Hamas once and for all;
The mission of Hamas is Israel's total downfall.
Hamas sees this as a chance to establish its place
As the Palestinian people's one and only true face.

Fighting continues; international pressure to no effect.
There is no end in sight to this costly conflict.
The Palestinian people will again suffer the most.
Will anything change when the sides give up the ghost?

Finger pointing has run rampant on both sides;
International news outlets spread each side's lies.
Compounded by politicians quick to assign blame,
They're prolonging this horror; the sides they inflame.

Finger pointing only assures more civilians will die
And the harder it will be to give peace talks a try.
Assigning blame is rarely helpful, it seems to me;
Please report only facts and the progress I hope to see.

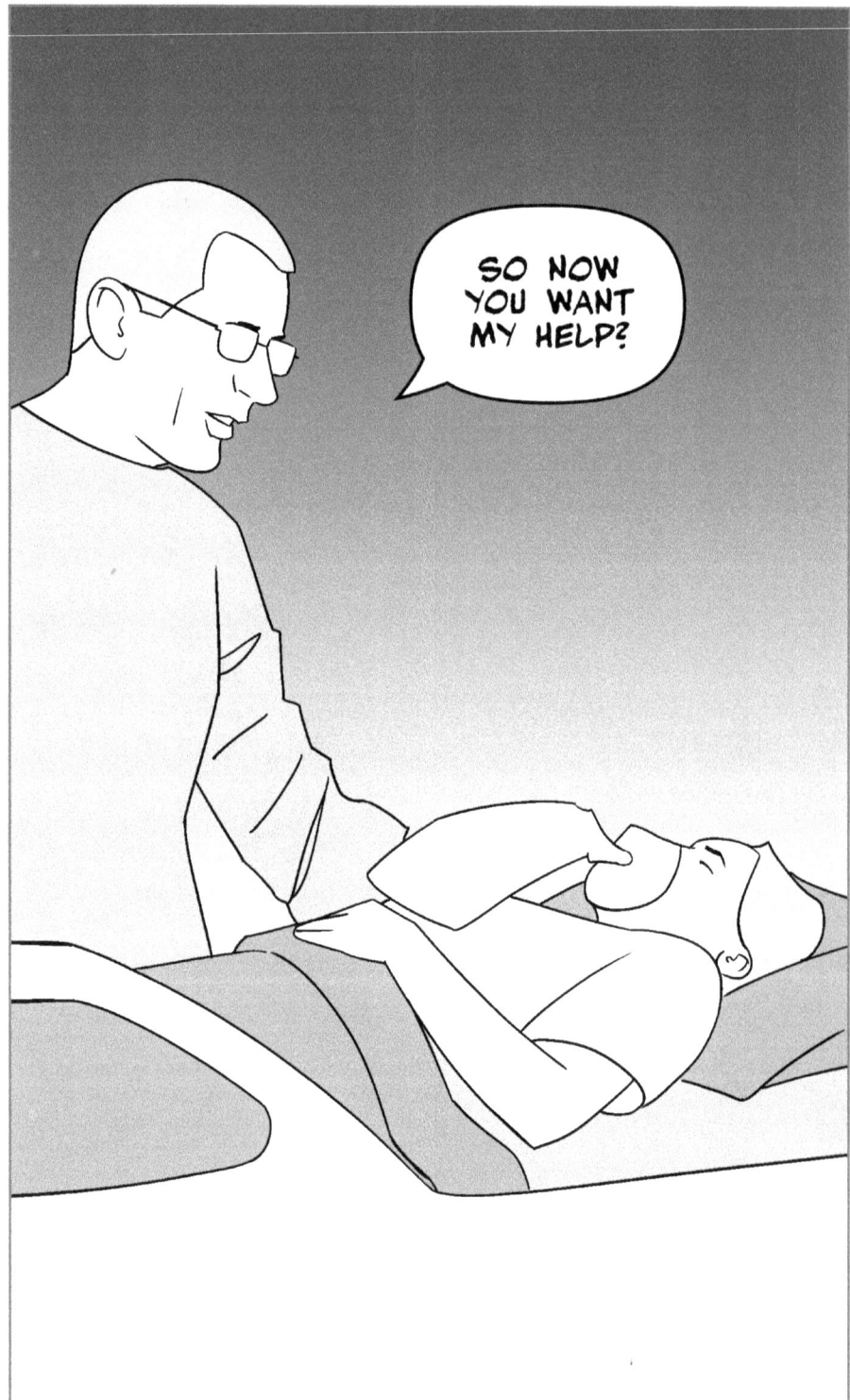

## Fauci — The Real Villain?

That dictator Fauci still demands we stay home,
That we mask, distance, and remain quite alone.
What diabolical reasons could there possibly be
To insist on restrictions and not set us free?

He says not enough of us are vaccinated yet,.
And the new delta variant is a formidable threat
It's doubling in cases, and the death count grows
If you believe his science, but what does he know?

The voices of reason are on the Republican side—
Voices like Senator Blackburn, Tennessee's pride.
She's called Fauci out, just a liberal mouthpiece.
So many proofs she's soon going to release.

Trump promised to fire Fauci when re-elected;
Biden stole our election, and to Biden, Fauci defected.
Is there any better proof which confirms that he's a fake?
Our freedoms as good Americans are at stake!

CNN and MSNBC, duped into airing "scientific" lies,
Republican views, Fauci and others criticize.
FOX never muddles their truths with fake news;
Their anchors present much more believable views.

Vaccinate, vaccinate—an endless refrain.
"Herd immunity" is what he wants us to gain.
He claims states near that "70 percent goal"
Have fewer cases, hospitalizations, and death toll.

Maybe it's true those vaccinated rarely get COVID-19,
But can't trust science, which changes so often it seems.
I'll not let Fauci dictate what I can and can't do;
I'll stick with FOX and not listen to the likes of you.

And speaking of that, will these libs never give up?
Demanding proof of vaccination, just to show up?
And businesses duped into playing their game;
Airlines, entertainment sites now doing the same.

Now he's trying to scare us with this new variant,
Claiming delta from India is even far more vigilant.
I've gotten along fine without a mask or a shot,
So I won't be buying into his nefarious plot.

I'll stick with Blackburn and friends on FOX news.
My freedoms are precious; those I won't lose.
So give up, Fauci. Stop leading the country astray!
But hey, please help me recover during my hospital stay.

## Is the Filibuster Rule Just an Evil Tool?

Most people know little about the filibuster rule
And its use as a defensive legislative tool.
Throughout the long history of its use,
It's often been the instrument of abuse.

The House has nothing like the filibuster rule;
It even seems to view the rule with ridicule.
The majority party in the House gets its say,
And no procedural rule stands in its way.

To the frustration of the House's majority party,
A bill they send to the Senate is no guarantee;
That's true whether or not their party's in control—
The opposing party can bury any bill in a hole.

Now here is the crazy thing about this rule
And why it's such an effective defensive tool:
Most bills require only a simple majority to pass,
But **to call a vote** needs three-fifths of the full Senate class.

So, just 51 votes usually needed to pass a bill;
Sixty votes needed to move it to a vote, if you will.
That's why its use is so very powerful to invoke;
Its declaration kills any bill with that one stroke.

Just Sayin 2021: A Perspective in Rhyme

Historically, filibusters were less effective than today.
Its proponent had to hold the floor, come what may;
And while in use, no other bill could be moved ahead,
Thus blocking all other business or bills to be read.

Today, personal appearance is not a requirement.
"Dual tracking" has eliminated the blocking impediment.
One party can simply say they are going to filibuster,
And other business can proceed without fuss or bluster.

The past 20 years have seen its increased use;
Usually the majority party will cite its use as abuse.
But truthfully, each party has used it to its own ends,
And the majority when the minority will employ it again.

I don't know whether it's a good or bad thing.
Historically, its use has left us with a terrible sting:
White majorities used it to deny Blacks' civil rights,
And today it's a tool in voter suppression fights.

President Biden, they say, doesn't want it eliminated
But rather see the original filibuster rule reinstated.
Senators had to stand there and talk until they collapsed—
Yes, tighten the current rule, which is too relaxed!

But obstruction remains the goal of the opposition;
Until the next election, delay will be their position.
And if the majority makes the filibuster go away,
The opposition will look for new ways to delay.

| Steve Rosen

But enough of this theoretical philosophy—
Here is today's sad political reality.
Dems will stop, wait, contemplate, and debate;
To reach its goals, Republicans will never hesitate.

# Infrastructure Bill, Any Chance?

Our infrastructure, so sadly overlooked,
Just a pawn in our politicians' playbook.
How sad since the need is so very great.
Another major disaster surely awaits.

Biden has made infrastructure a priority;
Clearly needed and a boost for the economy,
Both Dems and Republicans see the need,
And Dems have clearly taken the lead.

Still, Republicans refuse to get on-board,
Claiming the Dems' plan, the country can't afford.
And so the parties parry around and around;
In the meantime, let's hope no bridge falls down.

Complicated,? Oh yes. The Dems are not aligned.
A 10-year, 3 trillion dollar plan, the House is behind.
That big spend gives some Senate Dems pause
While other Senate Dems fully support that cause.

And let's not forget McConnell's vow
To thwart the Dems' every initiative somehow.
So though Republican states have many needs,
A Biden priority, McConnell refuses to concede.

As of today, 7/10, the discussions go on and on...
The press reports "progress"; each party's pawn.
Now two bills would require a compromise;
If tied together, no chance, not a surprise.

It seems the only chance there is for "success"
Is a targeted infrastructure bill for a trillion or less.
If passed, the Dems could claim a priority victory
If progressive Dems would just let that result be.

Republicans could brag they reigned the Dems in
And tout the funding as a Republican win,
And each party could move on to the next fight,
Each declaring victory to their supporters' delight

But alas, as of this writing, I fear it is not to be.
Dems in Congress seem unwilling to accept reality.
If Joe, Nancy, and Chuck can't forge a compromise
That failure may well be their majority's demise.

## Anti-Vaxxers, Not Helping

I'm not making this up; Trump did get the shot!
He really did; it wasn't a liberal propaganda plot.
And his kids, his wife, and his close aides, too.
That's what sensible, responsible people do.

I know there is history to vaccine hesitancy,
But that's a total myth, not a bit of fact, you see.
For decades, vaccinations were the accepted norm;
Getting your childhood shots was good form.

Shots cause autism; well, that's been proven untrue.
They're experimental; yes, but tried and true.
Some have died; but more than 99 percent have not.
Some get the virus anyway…but milder with the shot.

With anti-vaxxers, it's clear logic and facts don't work.
It's all emotion; give them logic, they go berserk.
Public opinion, vaccine campaigns sway so very few;
To attain herd immunity, curtail the surge, what to do?

My ignorance, thinking anti-vaxxers were very few,
Limited to some religious sects; that's just not true.
They're international, organized, and show determination,
Defending their right to choose over any vaccination.

So as we move towards the end of July,
The Delta variant has increased cases sky high.
In every U.S. state as more and more people die,
Still the unvaccinated won't give shots a try.

Evidence is everywhere of this variant's effect,
More contagious and sometimes hard to detect.
The data shows the newly infected are persistently,
Overwhelmingly, the unvaccinated predominantly.

Around the world, the evidence is much the same:
Increased cases, renewed restrictions, a shame.
In Japan where the Olympics are about to begin,
Stadiums are silent; no patrons will be allowed in.

Republican leaders support the anti-vaxxers' cause
By their silence or sometimes forceful applause.
FOX News spreading vaccine safety lie after lie,
A main reason anti-vaxxers won't give shots a try.

In California, new mandates for masks were put into effect
Helpful? Maybe, but beyond California, not much else yet.
Red states are where most new cases seem to be;
Judging by their history, no mandates there you'll see.

Those Red states have the lowest vaccination rates.
No wonder, no surprise those high cases are their fate!
Even Blue states are reluctant to re-employ controls;
Restrictions were just loosened up there on the whole.

To summarize, I'm not seeing a lot of cause for hope.
In fact, we are sliding further down a slippery slope.
The fall and winter are not that far away;
Higher vaccination rates would help save the day.

"Don't dictate, take my freedom"; you hear that a lot.
They're sincere and don't want to be put on the spot,
But don't they wear seat belts and follow traffic laws?
Somehow they don't see their position is flawed.

Listen up, anti-vaxxers: Shots are the right thing to do.
Do it for yourself, your families, and the country too.
Don't listen to FOX, to Biden, the web or even to me.
Remember, it's Trump's vaccine; it's safe and totally free!

# Apartheid, U.S. Style

We're witnessing a Republican version of apartheid,
Using any means to hold power. That's right,
An aging white majority base, the core of their power;
Support for white supremacists strengthening every hour.

Apartheid didn't work in South Africa, but can it work here?
Sadly, that fall took a struggle and too many years
The white supremacist movement is strong and on the rise;
Following Trump's lead, they are empowered, no surprise.

The January sixth riots evidenced their rage;
A forceful show of white power, they staged.
Fearing a Biden win might usher in their end,
A call to arms to their base they sought to send.

Biden was confirmed notwithstanding that assault,
That vote Republican Congressmen tried to halt.
Failing that, they set a new coordinated plan of attack,
Using any means to hold the minority vote back.

State laws passed suppressing voter access and registration,
Claiming widespread election fraud as their motivation,
Efforts by Dems in Congress to pass a national voting law
Filibustered; claiming voting was a province the states oversaw.

As of this writing, I can't see voter suppression efforts end.
Is it the formula that puts Republicans in power again?
And if those efforts result in wins in the 2022 elections,
What might they do next to advance minority suppression?

# "Andrew Two" — So Sad; You're Through

When last I wrote, I said I would wait and see;
Clearly, events have now overtaken me.
Eleven women accusers spanning many years;
Doubts I may have had now have disappeared.

Letitia James led a five-month detailed investigation,
The results, so condemning, require little explanation.
Almost 200 interviews underpin the results;
Cuomo excuses now seen mostly as added insults.

Through it all, Cuomo steadfastly refuses to resign—
Excuses, not apologies, he's given for his "crimes."
Criminal charges are under review in four NY counties;
Impeachment may await him in the state assembly.

It appears he wants his day (or two or three) in court,
Hoping the evidence against him falls short.
But as unlikely as the chances of that may be,
His defiance may force those inevitabilities.

But there is another aspect of this intriguing case:
It's how quickly he's fallen from grace.
The president, governors, senators are just a few,
So many saying, "NY must be done with you!"

What's special about this group's public outcry?
They're all the top leading Dems, that's why.
I can't, can you, think of any single time
Republicans called out one of theirs for a crime?

The results of this probe are just four days old;
There may be much more of this story to be told.
For the time being, I'm again going to wait and see
If coming events warrant an "Andrew Three."

## Postscript

On August tenth, Cuomo gave up the ghost and resigned;
I'm not giving this saga any more of my time.
Fittingly, maybe ironically, the next governor will be
Kathy Hochul, the first female governor of NY, you see.

One final twist to the story of some note:
James, who led the investigation, now seeks that post.
Was she unbiased in the work she undertook?
I'm sure we'll hear more about that in coming books.

# Will Delta Be the Worst? / Will Boosters Save the Day?

Throughout the country, Delta cases are growing.
No surprise, hospital beds are overflowing.
It's the same the world over, every place that you go,
And as of now, there is no indication it will slow.

Corona is making life quite scary once more;
Delta is raging worse than any strain heretofore.
We've lost the race to achieve herd immunity;
We're now experiencing a 50-state calamity.

Back to where things were 18 months ago,
In the midst of a foreseeable ongoing horror show,
Our collective failure to reach herd immunity
Has allowed Delta to flourish constraint free.

Cases are overwhelmingly worse in those states,
Evidencing vaccine hesitancy and low vaccination rates.
Ninety-five percent or more of new COVID cases
Are the unvaccinated taking most hospital places.

Those few vaccinated who still do become ill
Mostly show only mild, or no symptoms, if you will.
But the data shows that breakthrough cases are increasing,
Which is why plans to offer a booster are proceeding.

Just when the country was on a path to normal,
The Delta virus has once again thrown us into turmoil.
Questions from a year ago, we're now facing again,
Like how to protect children with school about to begin.

The same leaders who were obstructionists before
Are ignoring the facts and denying once more.
DeSantis is clearly the worst of that obstructionist lot;
He has single-handily put Florida in a precarious spot.

Now the CDC is recommending a booster shot.
This is an about face; something we've seen a lot.
You see, some time ago, Pfizer announced a booster;
The CDC responded, "Thanks—maybe in the future."

Not long after, Israel announced their booster plan
To provide a third shot to everyone that they can,
They were seeing the increase of case after case
Of sick, fully vaccinated people at an alarming pace.

That data in addition to the spread of Delta here
Led the CDC to modify its advice and change gears.
Those immune-compromised should get a third boost;
For the rest, well, no need for a booster to be used.

Was it a week or two, or just a mere few days,
When the CDC changed advice in a dramatic way?
A booster shot now recommended for everyone,
But not until eight months after your last one.

What's the logic behind the eight-month delay?
The current data shows a shorter effectiveness decay.
Most folks will ignore that advice from the CDC
And decide to get a third shot expeditiously.

Third shots won't solve the anti-vaxxer persistence.
Despite some inroads, there is still much resistance
Will that resistance facilitate yet another new strain?
Will all our efforts to fight COVID have been in vain?

Dr Fauci is out with a new truly dire warning.
Delta is marking time for a new variant to be spawning,
One more potent that will evolve into a greater threat,
More spreadable and deadlier than anything we've seen yet.

Every day, we learn more and more terrible facts:
Young, sick children infect you if you interact;
Deer and other animals proved to have the virus,
Soon it may be shown that they can transmit it to us.

Will the government realize enough is enough?
Take the difficult steps and once again get tough.
Experts don't believe the virus will just go away;
Strong action is needed, or a price we will pay.

The question I have is why we seem to never learn
Will we wake up before we reach a point of no return?
COVID, the climate—pick your end of life catastrophe.
Sadly, we keep putting off addressing these realities

# Afghanistan – The U.S. Is on the Run

Let's start back to when and where it all began:
9/11/2001 events led us directly to Afghanistan.
Following the horrible events of that day,
We were determined to make al-Qaeda pay.

First, we needed the Taliban to be on the run,
A necessary first step to seeing al-Qaeda undone.
al-Qaeda was receiving sanctuary in Afghanistan
Being sheltered by several Taliban tribal clans.

It took several years to finally root al-Qaeda out;
They re-established in Pakistan without a doubt.
Osama bin Laden was caught there, made to pay,
Almost 10 years after 9/11 on a 2011 May day.

We stayed in Afghanistan, as we stayed in Iraq,
To try to establish democratic building blocks
To allow women and girls the freedom to pursue
Education and careers like Western women do.

A U.S. military presence to keep the Taliban at bay,
Trained an Afghan army to be their mainstay,
Established a central government in the city of Kabul,
First Karzai then Ghani as president; American tools.

With al-Qaeda gone, the Taliban re-emerged
Determined to see Western ideas purged,
To return strict Sharia law to Afghanistan,
And to that end, do everything they possibly can.

So this struggle between ideologies raged on
For 10 more years; no quit in the Taliban.
And over that total of 20 long years,
More than 2,000 U.S. soldiers died, to be clear.

Trump negotiated a peace with the Taliban;
Biden promised that deal would actually get done,
Which leads us to the current events of today
And those horrific TV images to all our dismay.

For how long could the Ghani regime last?
Came as a huge shock when it crumbled so fast.
President Ghani was one of the first to flee,
Followed by a quick surrender by the Afghani military.

What fate for those looking West left behind?
The Taliban promised that they will be fine,
That theirs will be a moderate Sharia law regime;
Their actions show a contrary position, it seems.

Who knows if Biden was properly prepared.
Could more Afghanis from the country been snared?
There are certainly an abundance of opinions being aired;
Investigations will assure that none of the guilty are spared.

Sensing weakness, Republicans tagged Biden a failure.
Republican politicians and FOX promising censure,
Criticism for poor planning and "friendlies" left behind,
While inciting fear: In your town, do you want "their kind"?

The saddest part of those leaders' behavior that I see,
Assigning blame is the only place they choose to be.
Horrific images played over and over for political gain…
Republicans denying history; their behavior a shame.

Benghazi, Benghazi, Benghazi; give me a break
The Republican's playbook; pounce on any "mistake."
We should demand from our leaders a better tone;
Constructive cooperation, the behavior they should own.

When the full story of the evacuation comes to light,
It will show that most of what was done was done right.
The largest peacetime evacuation undertaken at any time…
Blame?  It's Republican rhetoric that's the real crime.

# Texas — You've Misread America's Pulse

Texas, along with Florida, leading the parade
To march democracy to its demise, I'm afraid.
A stolen election Republicans would have us believe,
Governor Abbott is leading the charge to deceive.

The Texas legislature moves in step with his plans:
Voting rights restrictions; a near total abortion ban;
An executive order banning mask mandates in schools,
Reckless at a time when we need anti-virus rules.

He's doubling down to ensure his initiatives succeed:
Bench warrants for Dem legislative "fugitives" decreed;
Legal filings up to the Texas Supreme Court,
Arguing mask mandate bans the Court should support.

Opposition is building within and outside the state,
Three important initiatives I'm most happy to relate.
Several cities are defying his order on mask mandates;
Those efforts are having some success as of this date.

The Justice Department is suing over the abortion ban,
Claiming it's "in open defiance of the Constitution."
The suit seeks an injunction to halt the Texas law
That allows any person to sue for violations they saw.

And while Texas was enacting these radical plans,
A recall of Governor Newsom was undertaken by Californians.
They had grown tired of virus mandates and restrictions,
So much so that his removal was a possible prediction.

The Texas abortion law became an issue in the recall;
A recall candidate, Larry Elder, an anti-abortionist after all.
Abortion rights advocates came to Newsom's defense,
The bid to unseat the Governor died as a consequence.

It's proof that Republican initiatives will rally opposition;
Florida is also experiencing backlash to DeSantis' positions.
Add Delta to the equation, surging, causing so much loss,
It may be that the Republican platform is their albatross.

# Infrastructure/Debt Ceiling – My Patience Tried

Infrastructure/debt ceiling issues are coming to a head:
One minute, some hope; the next both issues are dead.
Secretary Yellen has set 10/18 as a firm date;
"Get the debt ceiling done or suffer a draconian fate."

The Dems appear to remain hopelessly in disarray;
Warring factions prevent them from finding their way.
Republicans seem content to just let the Dems fight;
Recent public polls seem to indicate they're right.

On the debt ceiling, Manchin and Sinema are a block,
Won't modify the filibuster; they'd run out the clock.
On infrastructure. there is very little progress I can see.
Progressives and conservatives continue to disagree.

As the months slip by, Biden's approval continues to fall,
Mainly because both of these issues continue to stall.
There is still fallout from the Afghanistan withdrawal,
But on that issue, public opinion seems positive overall.

So as of now, this country may see a default, a first;
As bad as that may be, I fear it won't be the worst.
Those Dem advantages in the House and Senate
In the coming midterms may take a big hit.

As obvious as that is to all the parties involved,
The Dems appear unable to get issues resolved.
My wife has similarly said this to me on occasion:
"It's their own damn fault if Dems hand over the nation."

## Update on the Debt Ceiling

On 10/7, both parties agreed on an extension bill,
The Dems in danger of losing their majorities still.
It's just a stopgap to bridge the government till 12/3;
Republicans are claiming the agreement as their victory.

The Dems are under more pressure than ever before,
Urgency now to increase the debt ceiling once more.
And now they're on their own to get something done;
McConnell has Biden, Schumer, and Pelosi on the run.

I may need to provide another update by year's end.
Will the Dems get a permanent fix or a stopgap again?
They look weak with every stopgap, and they can't just postpone;
Weaker still if they need Republicans to throw them a bone.

# An Early Test of the 2022 Elections

Virginia has one of two statewide elections this year;
The policies tested will influence 2022, to be clear.
The Virginia race for governor may show Trump's power
And possibly the dawn of the Dem's dark hours.

McAuliffe, the Democrat, wants to distance from Biden,
As Biden's approval rating is slipping again.
To counter, McAuliffe brought in some heavy hitters:
Obama, Warnock, Ossoff, Abrams, proven vote getters.

Glenn Youngkin, the Republican, seems tied to Trump.
Trump endorsed him; is that one he'd rather dump?
In recent years, Trump's Virginia popularity has waned.
Many statewide legislative seats, the Dems have gained.

Each candidate has baggage to discount, to ignore,
While tying the other to leaders their voters deplore,
Using issues at the forefront of national debate
To tie each other to positions their supporters hate.

The issues that are the major Virginia political themes
Are the same ones in the national mainstream:
Media coverage on abortion, COVID, voter suppression…
Each candidate uses these issues to win voter attention.

Compare Virginia to New Jersey, the other statewide race,
The same issues and party strategies are firmly in place.
Though New Jersey is a more Democratic leaning state,
Voters views on these issues will be important to rate.

Viewing these issues on their importance to voters,
The Texas antiabortion law has each side's supporters.
The anti-abortionists are mostly on the Republican side;
Pro choice, mostly Dems—women must have the right to decide.

Voter suppression, too, is an issue with a clear divide:
Republicans restrict access; fair access, Dems provide.
Will these issues be important in choices voters make?
Only if voters believe changing the laws is really at stake.

COVID issues divide voters the least along party lines;
They could be very persuasive in young voters' minds,
Tired of mandates more than any group of voting age
But clearly not alone in wanting to turn the page.

Emotions run high for mask and vaccine mandates;
For indoor venues, these are restrictions many hate.
It seems as soon as restrictions finally ease up a bit,
The "state" reimposes them for our collective benefit.

I'm eager to watch polling as Election Day grows near.
Which issue(s) will emerge catching voters' ears?
Or perhaps be surprised as some new issue holds sway;
The parties eyeing 2022 will watch closely Election Day.

I hope that what comes out of this Election Day
Is a clear message to Trump, nothing halfway:
"Your "influence" is over; America wants you away";
The vote, a referendum putting Trump out to stay.

# Post-Election and Looking Ahead

It's November third, and the 2021 elections are over,
Not clear if there is a path for the Dems to recover.
For sure the Dems have suffered a big time loss,
Partly due to voters thinking little of Biden as a boss.

An issue that I highlighted in my writing above
Are the restrictive mandates voters want nothing of.
Will politicians in blue states now loosen mandates?
Will that lead to another round of virus outbreaks?

Ciattarelli modeled himself after Trump and lost;
Youngkin, who distanced from Trump, will be the boss.
McAuliffe, focused on the evils of Trump, not much more
Was rejected by voters who showed him the door.

Republicans focused on basic issues, like education;
They used critical race theory to stir voter attention.
Dems having their major initiatives in Congress stalled
Clearly found themselves with their backs to the wall.

Republicans have successfully energized their base,
Gained from suburban backlash regarding critical race.
Cancel culture, progressive ideas, maybe have gone too far
For 2022; it's the Republican formula and sets a high bar.

After the elections, Dems passed an infrastructure bill;
A few more wins, maybe they can salvage 2022 still.
But Republicans now have a strategy of their own;
Their game plan is to ride those issues into the end zone.

In 2022, progressives will remain targets of Republican ire.
If Dems don't moderate, their election results may be dire.
Sadly, I don't see AOC or her progressive House mates
Moderating their behavior, thus sealing the Dems' fate.

But don't Manchin and Sinema share the blame?
They held up passage of Biden's agenda just the same,
And Manchin resisted any change to the filibuster rule.
Wouldn't that rule change have been a helpful Dem tool?

Fair points, certainly their obstinance held up both bills,
But their positions seem in keeping with voter goodwill.
The progressives would like them brought more in line,
But would less progressive influence serve Dems just fine?

I hope President Biden reads the writing on the wall
As he and the Dems look to the elections next fall.
Most Americans favor the "build back better" bill;
Sell it, but distance it from the work of progressives' will.

On November fifteenth, Biden signed the infrastructure bill;
With bipartisan support, it had plenty of resistance still.
Thirteen progressive House members refused to sign on,
Still demanding it be used as a build back better pawn.

Republicans in Congress came to the bill's aid,
Recognizing its value to their states, but a price they paid.
Immediately they were assailed by Trump for their position;
They had committed the "first sin"—aiding the opposition.

Some subjects I've not covered like, the 1/6 Commission;
Not discussing it was by design and not an omission.
Aside from issuing subpoenas, they've done little to date,
So as with some other developments, I'll just wait.

There are the current and looming 1/6 defendant trials.
Many admit guilt; blame Trump; but still a few denials.
Too little remorse for what they did that day,
Most verdicts were guilty; they're being jailed away.

The Kyle Rittenhouse trial grabbed media attention,
Reminding us of the 2020 anti-police demonstrations.
He shot two demonstrators dead in Kenosha that day.
He had no business there; they acquitted him anyway.

November seems the month for social justice trials;
Many of them had a religious or racial bias profile.
One of the worst was the murder of Ahmaud Arbery,
A case dating back to a year ago in February.

Authorities in Georgia took too long to bring a case
Despite viral videos documenting his death, such a waste.
Three white men chased and hunted Ahmaud down;
One shot him, then cursed him while on the ground.

### Postscript to the Ahmaud Arbery Matter

Found guilty on all counts; fallout abounds.

Late November, the House passed the build back better bill;
Now off to the Senate, it's in for a battle still.
The 51 Senate votes needed may be hard to find.
Is there a compromise all the Dems can get behind?

On 12/3, Congress passed a stopgap funding bill;
The government gets to keep running until 2/18, but still,
The parties will again have to dance the dance before that date;
No chance that by then Republican obstruction will dissipate.

### Cuomo Saga Update

Chris, on CNN, had stated he was going to stay out of it,
But one of Andrew's supporters publicly let it slip
Chris tried to use his resources, went behind the scenes,
To uncover anything helpful to his brother he could glean.

CNN, having learned of Chris' secret brotherly aid,
Has now suspended Chris from his job, so well paid.
Mario, for sure, must be turning over in his grave;
This is certainly not the way he taught either son to behave!

This may prove to be a bigger story than Chris or Andrew.
It casts a cloud over all CNN reporting, all that they do.
It's well known that FOX is biased and outrageously untrue;
It would be unfortunate if CNN gets tagged with that label too.

## Postscript

On 12/4, CNN fired Chris Cuomo.

## Will Roe Be Undone by Mississippi?

Simply put, Roe prohibits abortions after 24 weeks;
Eighteen weeks is what the Mississippi anti-abortion law seeks,
But Roe has been the law of the land since 1973.
Politics, the only reason to overturn that long standing decree.

On 12/1, arguments were held before the U.S. Supreme Court;
Those for and against abortion gave their side vigorous support.
The six conservative Court members signaled a probable ascent,
A clear indication that they would not be bound by precedent.

We won't know the Court's decision until next year in July,
But from now until then, an easy prediction—the fireworks will fly.
And with midterm elections also set for the end of next year,
The abortion issue will be a major driver of the vote, it's now clear

## What Next?

Twenty-twenty-two is promising to be a stormy year—
The far right and far left will be more combative, I fear.
The midterm elections are fueling radical political activity;
Gosar, Boebert cases in point; how more crazy will it be?

# One Final Note

While writing about 2021, one theme became clear:
As Biden began his first full presidential year,
Republican obstruction was certainly expected;
All Dem initiatives, Republicans would ensure got tested.

All the Dem in-fighting, I didn't foresee,
Or Biden's approval numbers falling so rapidly,
Nor could I have known of Cuomo's fall from grace
Or the Afghan government's fall at such a quick pace.

Israelis and Palestinians—fighting erupting again;
I had no clue it would be this year… Will it ever end?
Of all the 2021 events in the news and in my thoughts,
The most surprising was COVID, the impact it wrought.

COVID is the subject of six entries in this year's work;
Blame Republican obstruction and anti-vaxxer jerks.
Obstinance caused us to fail to reach herd immunity,
Allowed variants like Delta and Omicron to evolve freely.

I never expected COVID to again dominate the news.
I thought, hoped by year's end, it would be through.
But instead, now before us and staring us in the face
Is another new variant spawning at an alarming pace.

The Omicron variant is spreading around the globe;
The EU and others are restricting travel, truth be told.
The U.S. stock market has started a predictable tailspin.
In 2022, COVID issues may well be dominate again.

So many unanswered questions it presents to us;
Will today's vaccines be effective against this virus?
Will it overtake Delta, be more contagious and severe?
There are so many aspects of this new virus I fear.

No one wants to face another year of this;
A year of COVID restrictions, we'd all gladly miss.
I hope when I write next year's end of year review,
There's lots of good news, and yes, COVID's gone too!

## About the Book

2021 was another volatile year on the political and social fronts. It was President Biden's first year in office, and while his administration attempted to legislate a new social agenda, it had to contend with the never ending fallout from the election and the prior Trump administration. Trump's "Big Lie" energized the Republican base and proved to be a force in the year long struggle between the parties.

Adopting a voter suppression strategy and sensing the country's unhappiness with the direction Democrat progressives were taking the country, Republicans set their agenda to win back Congress in 2022 at any cost.

And throughout the year, the COVID virus, it's mutations, vaccine hesitancy and mandates proved challenging for the Biden Administration, adding another dimension to the struggles between the parties.

## About the Author

Steve is a retired attorney who lives with his wife Marilyn of 50-plus years in their longtime residence in New Jersey. Together, they have two children and four grandchildren.

CPSIA information can be obtained
at www.ICGtesting.com
Printed in the USA
JSHW022145141022
31575JS00001B/14